Homegrown

and other poems

Enjoy the ride

Bryce Burnett

by **Bryce Burnett**

DriverWorks Ink

Library and Archives Canada Cataloguing in Publication

Burnett, Bryce, 1950-, author
Homegrown : and other poems / by Bryce Burnett.

ISBN 978-1-927570-08-1 (pbk.)

1. Cowboys--Poetry. 2. Ranch life--Poetry. I. Title.

PS8603.U73787H64 2014 C811'.6 C2014-901665-4

Editing and book design – Deana Driver, Al Driver
Cover and inside photos by Bryce Burnett except where noted

Printed on recycled paper.

Printed and bound in Canada.

Contact Bryce Burnett:
306-773-7065 www.bryceburnett.com

DriverWorks Ink

DriverWorks Ink
110 McCarthy Blvd. N., Regina, Saskatchewan, Canada S4R 6A4
www.driverworks.ca (306) 545-5293

Contents

Dedication

This book is dedicated to
the memory of my father and mother,
David and Dorothy Burnett,
who exposed me to their values of life,
challenged my dreams
and
inspired my imagination;
also
I am honoured to acknowledge
Deana and Al Driver
from DriverWorks Ink
as publishers and new-found friends.

Introduction

The poetry between the covers of this book is a selection of writings which highlight life on the Prairies of southwest Saskatchewan. Featured are poems depicting memories and stories of settlers, homesteaders and characters in our region, who have come before us and courageously set the stage for our very existence.

As I look throughout my community, I find it disheartening that many stories and memories have been buried along with the old-timers who created them. With that in mind, many of my poems reflect community events and happenings that I recollect from my growing-up years. I have included, with pride and honour, memories of my mother and father – parents who were similar in nature to many of those who have stamped their values on the growing communities of the Prairies. Although they are no longer at our side, reflections of them and memories of their love and caring for their family have been implanted in me and are an inspiration to pick up pen and paper.

In many poems, I pause to take time to remember where I came from, where I am, and where I am going; I just ain't in a real big hurry to get there. So as you settle into my saddle, just loosen off the cinch a tad and enjoy your ride in my world of cowboy poetry.

Prospectors Of The Prairies

At the turn of the century – and that's the 20th century for you younger folks – many homesteaders found their way onto the prairie soil of the great Canadian West. Such began the adventures of my grandparents. In 1901, my grandfather Walter Burnett ventured here from Scotland and herded sheep for the 76 Ranch. In 1907, Walter and Jane Burnett homesteaded the land where my family and I now live. My grandfather Jack Pendleton, at the tender age of 15, arrived here from Ohio in 1906 and homesteaded on the rich prairie soil. I have been privileged and am proud to farm and ranch on the land that both my grandfathers homesteaded.

I have had the good fortune of accompanying my father, David Burnett, on many a visit to pioneers of the Prairies – the farming couples, bachelors, and old-timers in our area. I reflect on days of simpler living when people realized life was a privilege; they shared and worked together out of both necessity and want. However, as years pushed on, rainfall diminished, dust storms prevailed, crops withered, cream cheques vanished and hard times became prevalent, it soon became evident that some were more privileged than others, maybe even by their own doing.

This section comes alive with poems of settlers, pioneers, old-timers and characters from diverse walks of life melding together in their quest for fulfillment as prospectors of the Prairies.

Tired Tribute

A tired tribute of the past tells tales of trial and toil.
When settlers ventured to tame this land, rolling over virgin soil.

Our pioneers wither and are falling fast, yet like this tattered wheel,
They were strongly built, hardwood to the core and banded with solid steel.

A sombre moment in time is like a broken spoke, shattered from grief and sorrow.
Too often, life spins much too fast, like there is no tomorrow.

The years roll by and clamour on like a wheel pounding the beaten trail.
As days push on and our forefathers fade, their strong spirits shall prevail.

Pioneer Haven

A castle piercing from the Prairie sky.
A monument crying out from days gone by.

Its boards once strong, straight and proud,
Embracing a pioneer couple in its shroud.

Once housing a family from harder days,
Memories all but lost to present ways.

A weathered victim of the harsh farming trade,
Where gardens grew and children played.

One family has gone, but she is still blessed,
When wayward critters seek a haven to rest.

Old-Timer

There was an old-timer lived out our way that I knew all of my life.
He was a man I admired; he raised a family, he and his loving wife.

As a boy, I used to tag along beside him on those hot summer days.
He showed me the value of work, the joy of play, and explained ranching and farming ways.

He taught me how to saddle a horse and throw a rope, and seed a crop of wheat,
How to shoot a gun, bait a fish hook, and at horseshoes I always got beat.

He was always there to give me advice whether I figured I needed it or not.
He taught me respect, steered me in the right direction, and helped me out of the odd tight spot.

Now as I've grown older, I've come to realize that the best compliment I've ever had
Is when an old-timer looks at me, smiles and says that I remind him of my dad.

Danny Bain

Danny Bain was a Scotsman who lived on the side of a hill.
He built himself a one-roomed shack; the impression in the ground remains still.

I remember one visit when I accompanied my dad to Danny's humble place,
He welcomed us in as reflections from his coal-oil lamp danced upon his face.

At a table in the corner, I sat in a rickety wooden chair,
The stove in the middle of the north wall warmed up the cool evening air.

And I recall how multitudes of newspapers were stuck to the west wall,
They offered a windbreak; after the news was read, the papers had another call.

The bed was tucked in the northwest corner, adorned by a big thick quilt,
This shiplap-boarded house was all he needed, a masterpiece he had built.

A carpenter by trade, he was always ready to give the neighbours a helping hand.
A bachelor he remained; he was but one homesteader who helped to tame this harsh land.

Chesters

As a boy, I enjoyed those special days when I'd visit the neighbours with my dad.
George and Edith Chesters lived down the road apiece, and a visit always made them glad.

On one quarter section, this English couple carved out a comfortable life.
There were many ways that old George kept busy when he was prodded by his wife.

George was equipped with a can of tobacco and some papers for a roll-your-own.
Edith enjoyed those soft taffy candies and the old dog, he just chewed on a bone.

In summer, they grew a huge garden and marketed much of their produce.
I remember the raspberries, as big as Dad's thumb; from the canes we pulled them loose.

When Dad hauled wheat, it always seemed there were a couple of pails' worth that never quite fit on the truck,
So we'd take them over to the Chesters to help feed their chickens; I'd watch them peck and cluck.

In the winter, Dad slipped over to see how they were wintering, about every second Sunday.
Out came the cribbage board; George's eyes glistened as he exclaimed "Bloody Hell!" when his cards he'd play.

I'd tag along with the Chesters to go fishing at Duncairn Dam on a hot summer day,
I'd ride in the back of that old Model T, and George stopped to fill its rad with water when we were about halfway.

We fished with frogs, sitting on five-gallon pails right on the edge of the water's bank,
When the day was done, he'd fill the truck with water; we'd jump in as he gave her a crank.

Now Edith looked forward to their trips to town; eggs, cream and garden produce they delivered around.
There was always time to visit Goodman's Studio and stop in at Max Johnston's on the way homeward bound.

It always amazed me how that old English couple possessed little, but had everything they did need,
Their lives seemed content; they held onto each other and never seemed to worry about what we call greed.

Bryce Burnett with George and Edith Chesters on one of many fishing trips.

George Law and Uncle Howard Hunter with a few of George's hounds.

George Law

This land was homesteaded by pioneers, with persistence in the opportunities they saw.
My father related to me stories of the old-timers, and especially one he called George Law.

Now Georgie immigrated to Canada to work for the 76 Ranch as a shepherd and hired hand.
Then he settled along the Swift Current Creek, naming his ranch after the Argyle hills of his bonny homeland.

He received a war pension of nine dollars a month plus every year, a new pair of boots.
A bachelor he remained in his one-room shack covered by hides of mink, muskrat and coyotes.

Now Georgie didn't need a lot, tobacco for his pipe, fresh water and a roof over his head.
One pan was used to wash himself and dishes, mix bread dough and, at night, it went under the bed.

Dad used to tell how as a boy he'd visit this old Scotsman on his favourite stomping grounds,
Lots of action pursued with his faithful horse "Bonny Boy" accompanied by at least a dozen hounds.

Now the neighbours didn't appreciate Georgie's dogs cause the odd chicken they were known to steal.
And when his truck appeared, hounds were packed in the front and back, but Georgie was usually the one behind the wheel.

Stories are told how Georgie went to town one day and ended up staying 'til late that night.
He mistook the railroad track for the road; having a rough ride, complained the road wasn't levelled right.

One day, Dad hired George to shingle the oil-shed roof, then off to the field he did run.
On his return at supper, George was standing, admiring the shed and what a great job he'd done.

Dad said, "George, look what you've done; you've got a shingle upside down in the middle of that roof."
"Don't worry, Davey. In years to come you'll say, 'That dirty old bachelor did that, but she's still waterproof.' "

George raised blood horses that were sure-footed and fast where only the strong prevail.
During one visit, Dad helped round up a band of these horses that were slated for a sale.

One stud singled out of the bunch and, after many times by the corral, that renegade's capture was grim.
Georgie appeared with a rifle; "Run him by one more time, Davey, and I'll take a shot at him."

George used to go to town Friday and on his return Saturday morning, he'd visit our house for a bit of a rest.
I remember him stopping by when we were ready to go to town, all dressed in our Saturday best.

George always had a Jersey Milk chocolate bar that he'd feed us one piece at a time 'til there was no more.
With our clothes covered in chocolate, Mother complained, never knowing where those dirty fingers had been before.

Men like George Law were the colourful pioneers who helped in the settling of this harsh land.
Their spirits live on although their memories fade as the time drifts along with the Argyle hills sand.

The Blister

In this journey through life, we've come to appreciate many a different kind of folk.
Cowboys come in all sorts and sizes, big and small, stern and jolly; some just like to joke.

There'll always be one old-timer, friendly as all get-out and sporting an old felt hat.
He's an enjoyable sort, always got a joke to tell and ready to chew the fat.

He's never in a hurry and likes to go fishing, especially on days that end in 'Y'.
The odd time, he even brings home a fish for his little wife to clean and fry.

At every sale or celebration, when they announce there's something free,
You're sure to find him first in line for coffee or a spot of tea.

He always stands right up in front at every closing-out auction sale.
He'll throw in the odd bid, but only buys if they'll toss in just one more pail.

He can tell the young buckaroos how it's done, throw a rope or stay on a horse's back.
But no one's seen him ride or bulldog a steer; he's getting old, so give him some slack.

He's a know-it-all, a one-of-a-kind, and just enjoys having fun.
He's known far and wide as 'The Blister', cause he never shows up until the work is all done.

Newlyweds

Uncle Howard and Aunt Agnes lived in the valley through which flowed Swift Current Creek.
Shortly after their marriage, they moved into a shack that was shingled from its base to its peak.

Now in that valley somewhat downstream lived an old bachelor, George Law.
He enjoyed a visit and was sure enough tickled about the new neighbours he saw.

Just before dawn, with much anticipation, to the newlyweds he made his way.
Upon entering their abode, he kindled a fire in the stove; the warmth would start their day.

The newlyweds awoke as the aroma of freshly perked coffee filled their humble house.
And there was Georgie, sitting at their kitchen table waiting, quiet as a mouse.

Howard and Agnes thanked George for his concern, then they tried to explain,
This was their home and he should knock on the door when he came calling again.

So a couple days passed; then as dawn broke, a banging came on their door.
Howard stumbled out of bed and there was George, ready to greet them once more.

They invited George in for oatmeal porridge and assured him they were doing okay.
Howard explained that George shouldn't arrive so early, but wait 'til they were awake and started their day.

After four days, they thought George must have gotten the message as he hadn't ventured onto the farm.
Then the next morning as light crept into their bedroom, goose bumps crackled on Agnes's arm.

She propped herself up from under the covers and her eyes gazed at what she'd surely regret.
For there was Georgie, peeking in the bedroom window, wondering if the newlyweds were out of bed yet.

Howard and Agnes Hunter raised three children in this humble home. Aunt Agnes took every day in stride and enjoyed visits from her nieces and nephews.

The Moose Hunt

The Jacksons were good neighbours, that's for sure; Inga liked to talk and Earl sure got his fill.
Earl loved to hunt and Inga was there to let him have it when he came home without a kill.

She only slightly complained when he went off hunting with the boys; after all, it's a manly sport.
It takes a macho man to kill a defenceless deer and brag how his shot was the deadly sort.

But Inga thought that things should change and the moose hunting party she would join one fall.
After all, she knew how to shoot, and a moose was a target big as a barn wall.

Earl argued, "That's no place for a woman; and do you even know what a moose looks like?"
Inga scoffed; of course she knew that species and she sure wasn't afraid of any wilderness hike.

So hunting season rolled around; Inga joined the hunt and into the bush she went.
With her 270 Savage and 180-grain bullets, she was scouting for a moose scent.

She'd show those men that she could shoot as straight as any man you know.
If she could just see a moose, she'd bag that thing; then those men could eat some crow.

Now Earl heard a couple shots ring out; it was Inga's 270 that had blasted those shots loose.
The sounds were a little to the west, so he headed out to see if she had bagged her moose.

When he arrived, there was Inga standing over her kill; he couldn't believe his eyes.
She was arguing with a cowboy, saying she'd shot that beast and he wasn't telling her otherwise.

She was going to tag it cause she knew she'd shot it, no matter
what that fella said.
That was her game; he hadn't bagged it, her 270 had nailed it dead.

Finally the cowboy said, "Okay, ma'am, you win," cause his ears
were starting to rattle.
"But before you tag my dead horse, would you please let me
take off my saddle?"

In 1935, my father, David Burnett was hired with his team of horses to lift up the lumber while Wyatt elevator was being built. In 1972, he watched it be demolished, as rural Prairie elevators became an icon of the past.

Grain Haulers

When I was but a lad, I liked to go along with my dad when it
was time for him to market grain.
I jumped in the old Chev, as its motor he'd rev, and we headed
out down the lane.

It was only a four-mile drive, but that road came alive as we
bounced down alongside the creek.
Then it was through Wyatt Coulee we steered that old dually,
and up to the elevator we'd sneak.

The elevator agent waved us ahead, as the truck barely sped,
and it then crept on to the scale.
Then he gave us a smile, saying, "I haven't seen you boys in a
while," as he grabbed a sample pail.

Over his glasses he strained as he moved weights on the beam
frame, and wrote down how much it weighed.
He said, "Let her go," and from the truck the grain did flow;
for Dad's hard work he was about to get paid.

The empty truck was weighed and a scale ticket was made,
then the agent gave us a goodbye wave.
From the elevator we parted, homeward bound we started,
the truck revived from the load it gave.

Those wooden elevators are gone that used to silhouette the
dawn and calmly bless the evening skies.
Only a boyhood memory remains of how I helped my dad deliver
grains to those country elevators of days gone by.

Grandpa Walter

It was back in the homesteading days, when sheep and cattle our pioneers did raise,
that from our family tree this story is a branch.
On a quarter section next to Yellow Lake, Grandpa Walter Burnett claimed his stake,
after overseeing a flock of sheep for the 76 Ranch.

The settlers were worried and there was talk about the coyotes being a threat to their stock
as lambing season was about to get underway.
So old MacKintosh a meeting he did call at the Yellow Lake Community Hall,
to discuss the overpopulation of the coyotes that day.

He said, "Our livelihoods we must protect; we could shoot those varmints or, better yet,
eliminate them with some poison bait."
Then a stranger said from a row at the back, "Fellas, give those coyotes some slack.
The species we just can't eradicate."

That government agent said they needed to study the situation of the coyote overpopulation,
so they concluded they'd reconvene with results in ten days.
Now that research team sleeked around on those southwest hills of the lambing ground,
to pursue the coyote and his menacing ways.

Well, the meeting date was a Friday night, and stockmen returned to the Yellow Lake site,
anticipating what the coyote study had revealed.
Eyes were on the government official that day, as he addressed the men and began to say,
"Boys, you're right; the coyote population has increased in the lambing field.

Fellas, we've developed a solution to decrease the coyote from their intrusion,"
as he explained how they'd address the situation.
"Now these coyotes we need to round up, and make sure to every male pup,
we apply the technique of coyote castration."

Walter Burnett stood up from a front-row chair, and in his Scottish accent he did declare,
"My gosh, sir, your remedy is a bit of a shock.
You see, you've delved into this matter much too deep; cause the coyotes are eating our sheep.
It's not that they're trying to breed our stock."

Best Buddy Glenn

I reached for the note that sat on the table, the words etched out with a pen,
"I'm sorry, dear, but I can't live here any longer – I've left with your buddy Glenn."

I stared at the note, trying to comprehend how things could have gone that far wrong.
I'd tried to provide for her the best I could, and Glenn was always there to help me along.

She had a nice house – at least it had running water; she had a car and a telephone.
And to run off with my best friend, how could this happen – he was always welcome in our home.

I recalled the time he and I embarked on a hunting expedition up at Loon Lake,
It was a great adventure and on our return home, he even helped her cook moose steak.

He and I explored many a lake and stream in search of that big fish day and night,
Then when we got home, he'd give my wife a hand, making sure they were cleaned just right.

And when business called me away, he'd take care of things and say, "Never you mind."
It set me at ease, knowing he was there to do chores when I left the ranch and my dear wife behind.

Now when your wife runs off with your best friend, it can surely bring a tear to your eye.
But you know the worst part about the whole deal is, I'm sure going to miss that guy.

Old Age

I met an old cowboy on the street the other day,
I believe he was a wine connoisseur.
As he lifted his head, he raised his hand with a bottle,
then looked at me with a blur.

He said, "Son, this getting old ain't what it's cracked up to be,
but it's part of nature's plan.
The years will go by and creep up on you, too,
so take care of your body while you can.

My back is sore, my head she aches,
and my stomach hurts with pain.
My eyesight isn't as sharp as it used to be
and this old toe swells up in the rain.

My legs won't bend like they did when I was young
as I climb up onto that saddle.
And when my old horse breaks into a trot,
my old bones shake and begin to rattle.

My joints, they creak; my muscles are weak,
and the hair is growing sparse on my chin.
My hearing isn't as clear as it used to be,
so mostly I just smile, nod and grin.

I'm sick and tired of being sick and tired;
my body has become outdated.
I've decided old age is like black cows and booze,
They're all highly overrated."

The Rock

I picked up a rock in the field the other day, and held it in the palm of my hand.
It was an Indian hammer head created by someone who before us roamed this land.

I wondered how it came to be abandoned there and whose hand had cradled it before I.
And I imagined what it had been used for and how many critters had passed it by.

Then I wondered how many hundreds of years it had laid there, or maybe a thousand or two.
And what did the fellow look like who lost it; did he resemble me or maybe you?

Then I noticed on my machine a tillage shovel was missing; I'd lost it in the field that day.
I knew I'd never find it; it was smothered with soil, abandoned somewhere it lay.

Then I wondered in a couple of hundred years or maybe a thousand or two,
Whose hand might reach down and pick it up; would he resemble me or maybe you?

And would he wonder how it came to be abandoned there and what the fellow was doing who lost it that day?
Would he imagine what it was used for, and why in the heck did they till the soil in this part of the world anyway?

Caboose

Days gone by and times to come are but for us to hold.
Every generation is concerned how the future will unfold.

Can our youth continue on and make this old world fly,
Will it be as great an era as those of years gone by?

Generations have flowed through time like a train travelling the track.
God in his greatness granted us insight to look forward as well as look back.

The future belongs to the young, and we must set them loose.
For if we cannot step aside, they'll run over our caboose!

Our son Wyatt and daughter Dena in front of the rail line going by the Wyatt elevator. The CPR kept the rail line open to haul gravel for a few years after the elevator was demolished.The elevator is gone, the rail line was lifted and now the roads are being worn down from hauling grain and gravel.

Roots, Reflections And Inspiration

It has been said that in order to know where we are going, we should know where we have come from. Reflections on our roots should give us guidance and inspiration; memories on which we can draw to fulfill and enrich our very being.

I, my brother and my sister were fortunate to have parents who cared for us in our growing-up years, gave their all to help us along, comforted us when we were down, celebrated with us in triumph, and pulled our ears when needed. Memories are strong of family involvement, as the actions of one member of the family sent ripple effects to the rest of its members. The branches of the family tree – although they all grew individual leaves – were heartily connected and intertwined, affecting and inspiring our tree's very existence.

By verse, we can cherish the memories of those we held dear – memories that grow stronger with the passing of time. It is sometimes the smallest of details that allow us to reminisce, kindle a smile and percolate the very essence of our roots. We may even recollect the smiles of our forefathers that relayed to us the pride and faith they instilled in us.

As you turn these pages, I invite you to reflect on your own roots. I hope you have fond memories, as I and my siblings do, of those who blessed us with such a wonderful beginning.

Family

We are the focus and the goal of every generation.
Truly the basic building blocks of our unfolding nation.

Standing steadfast side-by-side in happiness and grief.
Respect, trust and understanding; true to our belief.

God placed us on this green earth to bind in joy and jubilee.
It is His plan in strength and love; the creation of a family.

A Tarentaise cattle family. It takes a lot of patience to get a photo like this one.

The Lips That First Touched Mine

The lips that first touched mine caressed
with care and yet of fear;
A tender moment of compassion,
strength and love so dear.

Those lips left an impression that would
persist throughout the years;
An imprint of caring, softly sealed with joy
and yet with tears.

Lips that overflowed with knowledge
and taught of right and wrong;
They spoke of truth and wisdom,
recited verse and sang sweet song.

Lips that taught of respect
and thoughtfulness, yet stern;
Gently pressed forth with support,
an embrace of no return.

As years press on, fond memories remain
stronger than none other.
The lips that first touched mine concealed
the love of my caring mother.

My parents, David and Dorothy Burnett, in their early days of marriage, pose at Swift Current's Frontier Days. Dorothy became involved with the Swift Current Agricultural and Exhibition Association which presents the annual fair. I am now on the board of directors of the Swift Current Agricultural and Exhibition Association.

Drugs

I blame my parents for the way I am and what I think and do today.
They were a catalyst in my drug addiction in every single way.

Its effects still flow here in my veins, and are stronger than heroin or cocaine.
Yes, they pushed me into my drug problem, and a strong craving does still remain.

It's all their fault; if not for them, I would have taken a different path.
Now the drug problem of my youth still haunts me, one of rejoice with little wrath.

You see, I was drug by my ear outside if I failed to finish chores in the barn,
And I was drug back in if the words I uttered were stronger than 'by gosh' or 'by darn'.

I was drug to the kitchen sink to dry dishes or even wash them if need be,
Then I was drug to bed by nine o'clock every night even though I begged to watch TV.

My hands were drug up and folded in front of me as my prayers they helped me say,
And we thanked God for our meagre fortunes and praised Him for every day.

Then in the morning I was drug out of bed with, "The early bird gets the worm."
Yes, I found worms and bugs and more when I was drug to that potato patch and a hoe put in my hands so firm.

Then on Sunday, I was drug to the old country schoolhouse; all the neighbours gathered there for church.
Later, Dad drug me to his favourite fishing hole, where we laughed as we caught some perch.

My mom drug me in and comforted me in those loving arms whenever I was feeling low,
Then she drug me off to swimming lessons – “You don’t want to drown, you know.”

One day, Mom drug two scrapping young boys outside and locked the doors; punishment for being a bad little tike.
That was the only time I can remember our house being locked; it was always open to friends and strangers alike.

The odd time I was drug into the corner and scolded, “You wait ’til your dad gets home.”
Then his heavy hand drug across my butt – polished her up like a piece of chrome.

Then his strong hands engulfed me, as he drug me close to his side.
Fond memories remain when he drug me hunting and fishing, or when we pitched those horseshoes and he laughed with pride.

Yes, my parents drug me through my boyhood years; they affected my behaviour in everything that I think, do and say.
And if today’s youth could have more of this type of a drug problem, I think this country would be a better place today.

Dad

As I walked across the yard the other day, I swear I saw my father.
Although he's been gone for many years, memories are stacked upon each other.

Sometimes it seems like only yesterday, other times perceive forever.
Those memories are so strong, I know they'll leave me never.

Yes, he gave me lots to think about – of right and wrong, the good, the bad.
And he showed me how this dirt would provide; he cared for the land, my dad.

As years go by, I catch myself doing things just like I know he'd done.
And sometimes my actions resemble his; I'm proud to be called his son.

Yes, I walked across the yard the other day and from my feet below,
I swear I saw my father; but alas, it was only my own shadow.

My grandparents, Frieda and John Pendleton, standing in front of their brick house. Jack, as he was known to neighbours, wore a crocheted sweater, which was a popular garment to Prairie folks.

The Crocheted Sweater

The old crocheted sweater still hangs in the hallway, even though ten years have passed.
It's right where he left it on that cool fall day, when chores were done at last.

She carefully hooked each stitch in place, to create that special present.
Her handsome man received the sweater; stitched on it a flying red pheasant.

He wore it proudly, that sweater crafted by the hands of his wife.
It kept him warm on frosty fall days and remained with him for life.

Man and wife married more than fifty years; years woven together with pride.
A lifetime of fulfillment, days of compassion and endurance side by side.

Now man and wife have both passed on, pioneers of the farming way;
But the sweater still hangs there in the hall, right where Dad left it that day.

Dorothy Burnett (Pendleton) started her career as a schoolteacher at Swinton School, located three miles from the Pendleton homestead and one mile from the Burnetts. Thus started the age-old story of the new schoolteacher being courted by the community's eligible bachelor.

Dorothy became involved in the community with the Swift Current Agricultural and Exhibition Association, Canada Day Committee, Wildlife Federation, hospital board, Regional Care Centre board, and the Swift Current Chamber of Commerce. In 1988, she was presented with the Order of Merit from the Swift Current Chamber of Commerce.

She is remembered as the elegant little lady with the sparkle in her eye and a smile as huge as the community she gave so much to and loved so dearly.

Mother

How do we describe a mother,
a single word that represents 'Mom'?
Is she the bond adhering the family together,
a place we come and go from?

Is the word nurture, security or comfort,
maybe free room and board?
Or her cuisine as a short-order cook, sandwich-maker
or the odd time, hospital ward?

She's a taxi driver, a cheerleader,
a loving smile on which we rely.
There to celebrate in triumph, console or punish,
a refuge for when we cry.

Yes, a mother is a teacher and preacher,
outfits us warm on a cold day,
Arms that hug us and hold us tight,
then guide us safely on our way.

Mom is forever in our thoughts to embrace us,
regardless how far we roam.
Yes, all these things describe our mom.
In one word, she is our home.

The Scotsman

I've got a tale to tell you about my dad, a Scottish man was he;
He took care of his pennies – some call it cheap, but I refer to it as frugality.

Now he was always ready to help out a neighbour and that's how our story does begin.
See, Jack Young cut himself bad on a sickle mower and his blood was a running thin.

He was rushed to the hospital and Dad went along to give a blood transfusion.
They had the same type of blood and with Dad's help, Young's life was saved from conclusion.

On their return home, Jack was overcome with compassion and as a gift, gave Dad a new shotgun.
He thanked Dad for sharing his blood and said without Dad, he surely would have been done.

Now a year went by and Young gouged his leg on some glass when he was thrown from his horse.
So it was back to the hospital and Dad went again – to give him blood, of course.

Jack was so pleased he had pulled through again; this Scotsman had saved his life.
So with gratitude, he visited Dad and as a gift gave him a new hunting knife.

Disasters happen and Jack Young was there when his old truck crashed into a tree.
He was cut up pretty bad and to the hospital transported, with a gash above his knee.

So for the third time, Dad shared his blood and the stronger Jack's life grew.
Jack sent a card to Dad for saving his life – it simply said, "Thank you."

That winter, the men talked over their common blood and how
Jack repaid Dad for helping so hard.
Dad said, "I don't understand; the first time you gave me a gun,
then a knife, and the last time just a card."

Jack Young's eyes sparkled as he said, "I know, and it might be
something I live to regret,
But you know, the more Scottish blood I gratefully get in me, it
seems the cheaper I get."

David Burnett, or Uncle D as he was known to his nieces and nephews, was a man of the land. Dave worked hard, then hunted and fished harder. He enjoyed family life, growing crops, working with horses and then machinery, and was extremely proud of the cattle we raised, showing them off to all who ventured into the yard. He was always there to help at community events, whether it was 4-H, tree-planting, pheasant-raising, picnics, reunions or auction sales. He was active with the Saskatchewan Wildlife Federation, trap shooting, and fishing contests. He collected old wrenches and enjoyed capping off the hunting trip with a draft of Hudsons Bay Rum – the darker the better.

Daddy's Hands

Daddy's hands were strong and firm, just like those of our great pioneers.
They worked hard to maintain the family farm, toiling throughout the years.

Many a day those hands worked from dusk 'til dawn, revealing blisters, bruising and pain.
They scooped up many a handful of dry farming dirt or lifted up, praising God for rain.

Yes, they were hands of a farmer who planted seeds and threw out bales of hay.
Those hands never failed to provide for his family as they worked hard from day to day.

My father David Burnett aboard a Massey Harris combine in the fresh air of 1957.

Yes, Daddy's hands were strong and firm as he harnessed Sammy and Dolly to the sleigh,
Those hands gripped the reins as horses thrust through snow, delivering to cattle their daily hay.

I watched Dad's hands as he milked old Bessie, putting milk on our breakfast table.
He grasped that hoe to weed hills of potatoes; full of blisters, but strong and able.

Yes, I admired Dad as he aimed that shotgun; his shots were straight and true.
He boasted he hit 50 straight when shooting skeet, a feat that's hard to do.

I watched Dad's hands rescue his faithful dog as it retrieved a duck from the ice cold river,
Then laid that dog by the stove and dried it with towels as its body shook with a shiver.

Yes, Daddy's hands were strong and firm as he pulled my ear to guide me in the right direction.
And I watched as he put his arms 'round my mother and those hands offered her affection.

I watched Dad's hands caress his grandchild and throw her in the air, to her mother's dismay.
With screams of joy as those strong hands cradled her; to him and her, it was nothing but play.

Yes, those hands grasped many a saskatoon tree and pushed pumpkin seeds into the ground.
Then they carved grandchildren's names onto those pumpkins that grew so big and round.

His hands caressed that favourite tool from his antique wrenches big and small.
They took perch off a hook, tapped maple trees for sap, and pounded cabbage for sauerkraut in the fall.

My dad, Uncle D, was fond of his nieces and nephews when they challenged him to pitch a horseshoe.
Then from his hands he'd offer them spearmint chewing gum – but only half a stick, mind you.

Those horseshoes were called many a name; as his hands pitched them, the harder they played.
Those shoes must have listened – each time they were cursed at, it seemed the more ringers they made.

Yes, those hands were hard and tough from a lifetime of toil, but still maintained a firm grip.
His handshake was true when a deal was complete, just as it was spoken from his lip.

Yes, Dad's hands were strong and firm, like his fellow pioneers who helped build this land.
They carved out a way of life in this farming community, always ready to lend a helping hand.

You know those hands lacked vigour as the years went by, but they always gave a friendly wave.
Yes, Dad's hands were strong and firm as they toiled hard but oh how much love they gave.

Those old hands are no longer here to help us along and keep us from going astray.
But the odd time, I feel them reach down from above to guide us all in the right way.

Man In The Mirror

I looked in the mirror the other day
and couldn't believe what I did see.
For there was my old dad behind that glass
just a staring back at me.

What happened to that young fella
who was there not that long ago?
Strong facial features, full of fantasy,
dreams and a youthful glow.

Yes, that old mirror reflected a few changes
through the passing years.
Yet the image is that of a family resemblance
through all the joys and tears.

Pretty soon my son will gaze in that mirror
and much to his chagrin,
It'll be my turn to play a trick myself
when I'll be grinning back at him.

My father's cousin William Burnett and my nephew William Burnett reflect on times to come and times gone by.

I've been told my grandfather Walter Burnett was proud of his Scottish heritage, as was my father David, and so it is with me. Grandpa Walter was a stockman, especially proud of his Clydesdale horses. His Clydesdales were Grand Champions at Frontier Days, Swift Current in 1920. Walter tended to his stock and kept in practice by herding Grandma Jane's flock of turkeys with his black border collie. Grandma kept turkeys, which put Christmas dinner on the tables of most neighbours every year.

My grandfather died before I was born. His border collie was by his side when my dad found my grandpa, collapsed from a heart attack while on the road to Yellow Lake. Does the destiny of one man shape the destiny of his progeny to follow? As one man's life fades away, does it pave a path to futures unknown? As we measure a man, can there be a prouder moment than the realization of knowing that the kindness in a man's heart is revealed by the faithfulness of his dog. That border collie lost his best friend.

The Measure Of A Man

How is it that we measure a man,
evaluate what his life is worth?
How do we define success,
how his life is valued from a humble birth?

Do we measure a man by religious beliefs
and by what his tongue does say?
Maybe it's by his work ethics
and how he spends his day.

Do we measure a man by his apparel,
in the cut of the clothes he wears?
Or by the grudge he carries on his shoulders
and the weight of the cross he bears.

Is success measured by the house he lives in
or by the truck he drives?
Or is it by the label of the Scotch he drinks
or that he's had five wives?

Do we measure a man by the money he makes
and how he flashes his diamond ring?
Or do we measure him by the size of his herd
or the size of another thing?

Yes, there's many a way to measure a man
and by the time on earth he does log,
But to my way of thinking, a lot is revealed
by the way that he treats his dog.

Our Brick House

Grandpa built it for a nickel a brick, back in 1928.
Then came the Dirty '30s, the stock market crash, the farming economy was dealt its fate.

Those strong brick walls sheltered seven Pendleton kids through their childhood days.
Then grandchildren explored its nooks and crannies, conquering its wondrous maze.

Throughout the yard, children scrambled, hiding in caragana trees.
Swinging from the airplane skeleton and on machinery scraped their knees.

Fast, furry rabbits were a challenge to catch, while the grey geese were well respected.
Parading African geese honked at intruders; that brick house was proudly protected.

The massive windmill pumped cool water where Grandpa Jack cleaned freshly caught fish.
And Grandma washed clothes, cleaned that brick house, and put porridge in Grandpa's dish.

Grandchildren chased around clean white sheets hanging on that wire clothesline.
Forts were built in the big wood pile – fuel for that brick house where we'd dine.

From the iron stove a fire roared, reflecting a sparkle on towering chandeliers.
The big chime clock ticked out loud, and rang off the hours into years.

Memories remain of Christmas, where tables filled that brick house from wall to wall.
Seating all the clan as Grandma said grace, humbly honouring her Saviour's call.

Many a night the evening lamp flickered as Grandma's Bible it was read.
She would calmly smile, thankful for each day, as she retired to her bed.

That old brick house still stately stands, reflecting memories of yesterday,
Of joy and struggles, a house filled with love, a church where Grandma faithfully did pray.

The Pendleton brick house built in 1928 remains a landmark in our community.

Crocuses

In the spring of the year, Mother Nature pushes forth, leaving Old Man Winter behind.
A new chapter is opened on the native prairie as purple crocuses from rich soil unwind.

A wave of blossoms, billowed by a warm spring breeze, softly signals the spring season,
With anticipation of a bright beginning, garnished in purple persuasion.

As a young boy, I gathered those flowers and presented to my mother a purple bouquet.
She would smile and say, "Aren't they pretty?" – placing them in a glass vase without delay.

Those crocuses brought my mother joy, placed on that kitchen table.
They signified the arrival of spring, like turning a page from a florist's fable.

Spring represents new life kindled from the fresh, rich, moist soil;
Special to my mother, as garden seeds were planted with joy and toil.

Now I still pick crocuses for my mom, although things aren't quite the same;
Cause now I place them in an earth-stained vase, right beside her name.

Father Becomes The Son –
Son Becomes The Father

It's been a few years over which many memories we did instill,
Days flourished with my father as his boots I tried to fill.

Many a day we worked and I watched that man as he explained the ranching ways,
And he cut a life out of the land his father homesteaded, in those harsh and unforgiving days.

I marvelled at that man as he helped me, and we carried that ranch along,
As the years went by and his body grew weak, his mind remained real strong.

One evening, Dad and I were checking cows going along the old Law place,
He opened the gate and as he tried to remount his horse, a look of despair came on his face.

For every time he'd put his foot to the stirrup, the horse'd move out of his way.
He said, "Old girl, what's wrong? What the heck's got into you today?"

I grabbed the reins and pulled her around as her hooves dug into the sand.
I said, "Come on, old man, get on up," as I reached out to give him a hand.

I grinned at him as his leg crossed the saddle; a distant look fixed in his eye.
He said, "I guess I'm getting too old; the years pass so quickly by."

And it was at that time that I realized the father had become the son,
And I myself had become like a father, helping him to get the job done.

Well, my father lived on that ranch until the year that he died,
And he taught his grandson to fish and shoot, and how to rope and ride.

You'd be proud, Dad, how your grandson's grown and taken a liking to the ranch.
He's a hard worker, Dad, and you'd be pleased that from your family tree he's a strong branch.

Now my son, he helps me with the ranch that I helped Dad with in days gone past,
And now I'm starting to realize that the years for me are also going by way too fast.

The other day, my son and I were driving along what used to be the old Law place,
I opened the gate and he drove that truck through as if he was in a race.

I closed the gate, then opened the door, trying to get my foot into the cab.
I swear they make these trucks too tall nowadays, as the seat I tried to grab.

My son reached over, caught my arm and said, "Come on, old man, get in."
Then I realized how times had changed, cause now he's the one looking at me with a grin.

As I closed the door, I felt a little moisture gather in the corner of my eye.
I mumbled under my breath, "My gracious God, how these years pass so quickly by."

David Burnett and his grandson Wyatt applying the brand to our cattle.

Community Connections

Throughout my growing-up years, our family relied on and helped with many events that took place in our community here on the Prairies. Families worked and played together, depended upon and relied upon one another for support when needed or not. Accomplishments and nourishment of the community resulted in a viable farming and ranching livelihood.

Communities flourished and overlapped one another. A good horse would get you most anywhere. A community was bound together by a Prairie elevator, one-room schoolhouse, community hall, church or the local general store. Most of these are pillars of the past, but memories still remain strong for those fortunate enough to have been touched by that era.

My father recalled that when he was a boy, the road going by our farm stretched for seven miles towards town. Along those seven miles lived seven families that farmed; produced grain, beef, milk, cream, pork, and chickens. They bought supplies in town and sent kids to school; they supported a community. Along that same road today lives only one old fellow who farms, ranches, and tries his pen at writing poetry. His wife nurses in town, puts food on the table and helps on the ranch. The ranch has been successful; the school bus no longer stops here, and neighbours along that seven miles no longer exist. Is that progress? You be the judge.

Community connections now require more than one good horse.

Homegrown

'Purchase your food locally' – that's a slogan we hear a lot nowadays.
And as a producer, I appreciate that, growing up in ranching ways.

I was born and bred right here on this ranch and I know the wholesomeness of it all.
We produce grain and beef on Canadian soil, and are proud we got that call.

I climbed into my tractor at haying time, got to keep my home-grown cows fed;
But as I looked out the windshield, a decal glowed 'Made in England', it said.

We're growing local produce with foreign machines; that label sure got my glance.
As I hooked up to the mower, a tag revealed that it was 'Made in France'.

I was thinking, "This isn't exactly right," then I noticed the baler came from the U.S.A.
Well, we're getting closer to home, but it's not quite the best way to make Canadian hay.

It sported an Italian driveshaft, and the bearings endorsed Mexico, if you please.
The chain links were stamped from Germany and the tires were Japanese.

I was thinking, "The rake will be different," but the plate showed 'Made in Italy'.
When I glanced at the metal draw pin, 'China' was stamped on it for all to see.

So here we are growing local food, all produced with foreign machines.
But what do I know, standing here in my field, dressed in Cambodian jeans?

Maybe I'm the only original on this ranch, where my parents worked and played.
So am I homegrown? Well, only Mom and Dad know if I can be certified Canadian-made.

Wanda and I, checking the cattle on our ranch in the Swift Curent area in 1995.
(Calvin Fehr photo)

Perfect Family Setting

The picture of a perfect family setting is easy to embrace;
One of the Christmas season and all the relatives, as smiles percolate on each face.

There's Mom and Dad, then Aunt and Uncle; by the brightly lit tree, kids and cousins explore.
Grandma and Grandpa burst in the door, with presents and gifts galore.

The turkey basted rich yellow and brown, scalloped potatoes smothered in cheese,
Are set upon the candle-lit table as Mom beckons, "Everyone, be seated please."

The relations scurry into their chairs, and Grandma is asked to say grace on this occasion.
She thanks our Lord for this great feast and his ultimate gift – the reason for our celebration.

Then Uncle exclaims, "Pass the spuds and from that cooked bird, please save me the heart."
Grandpa turns to his grandson and says, "Pull my finger," then he lets out a resounding fart.

Now Aunt says, "That's disgusting." Kids laugh and giggle with glee;
Mom is embarrassed, Grandpa's relieved, and Dad's thinking, "Better him than me."

Grandma says, "You old fool, that'll be enough out of you today."
Cousins fan the air, then Uncle says, "Where's those sweet spuds anyway?"

Now family get-togethers can be unforgettable; many we remember just because;
But if this doesn't depict a family setting, then you tell me what the heck does.

Stockman's Apparel

A cowboy hat, a sisal rope, underneath the scuffed old boots;
These are the basic stockman's apparel; you could say they are his roots.

The hat sets upon his head to cap his very top;
It screens the sun and offers shade for his sparse hair crop.

Around his feet, the boots caress, and with their very sole,
They keep his toes from aches and pain as cowhide leather takes the toll.

But this old rope, what is its role? Don't let our cowboy fret;
As he grows old and his belly sags, we'll cinch him up with this lariat.

Steps

These are the steps to nowhere,
where no one ever goes.
These are the steps of days gone by;
the steps our pioneers bravely chose.

These are the steps the workers climbed
to pile hay the farm did grow.
They are the steps the farmer scaled,
then fed his livestock down below.

These are the steps the wife peered up,
calling, “Kids, get down from there!”
These are the steps the collie bound up,
and steps the daughter used as a chair.

These are the steps that Grandpa climbed
to survey the property from the loft.
And stairs that Grandma struggled up,
kittens cradled in her apron soft.

These are the steps the children clamoured up
to romp and play in the hay.
And these are the steps the grandchildren climbed
to explore the loft one day.

Now these are the steps to nowhere,
where no one ever goes.
Yes, these are the steps of days gone by,
an era that’s come to a close.

Here, I am reciting poetry in the church at Doc's Town, Kinetic Park – home of Frontier Days, Swift Current. My father-in-law, Woodrow Newton, was raised and lived on a ranch near Hallonquist, Saskatchewan. He related this story to me many times. He claimed the incident happened at the local church in Hallonquist. After Woodrow passed away, this story haunted me. I thought it was a classic, so I put it to verse. So did it actually happen? Well, it could have. Maybe it did. Probably not; but it sure makes for a great story.

(Prairie Post photo)

Cowboys And Church

A cowboy and church aren't overly compatible.
It's not that he doesn't believe in God and His word.
The Almighty summoned Mother Nature to ride alongside the cowboy,
just as he vigilantly watches over the herd.

Now a cowboy ain't fond of crowded spaces,
starched collars, windsor knots, and ties,
And sitting quietly in church can be somewhat uncomfortable,
especially if his pants are stuck tight to his thighs.

Well, one Sunday morning the minister asked us to rise,
and sing glory to God up above.
In front of me was a lady with the pleat of her dress disappearing
as if sucked in to fit tight like a glove.

It looked uncomfortable as hell, how that dress seemed to be
stuck up there between her two cheeks.
And she started to wiggle a bit to loosen the garment,
causing the pew to give off a few creaks.

Well, I thought it only right to lend her a helping hand
so I reached out and gave a tug on that grey dress.
There was a quick release as it came out of that crease,
and she was relieved of her terrible distress.

Now as she peered around, I gave her a smile,
acknowledging that everything was now alright.
But by the scowl on her face and as she shook her fist,
it was evident that not only her dress was uptight.

Her red face blurted out words that you shouldn't hear in church,
as she began to cuss and curse.
I started begging for mercy, when around came her left arm
and caught the edge of my eye with her purse.

I muttered, "Sorry, madam," as I begged and I pleaded,
realizing I'd done something terribly wrong.
"I should have left the dress the way it was," I thought to myself,
as the choir broke out in a Praise the Lord song.

From my swollen eye I peered; it had looked uncomfortable to me;
but maybe that's the style for a grey dress edged in green.
So I cautiously reached out and, with the edge of my hand,
tucked that dress right back the way it had been.

Well, you guessed it right; it was that day in church
that you might say all hell broke loose.
When a lady in a grey dress tucked tight up her butt
flew around like an old mother goose.

So a lesson to you men – sometimes a lady doesn't want a helping hand,
no matter how hard you might try.
And women, remember – a man can't give you a proper hand
if his vision is blurred by a black-and-blue eye.

The One-Room Schoolhouse On The Prairie

The one-room schoolhouse on the prairie stood proud for all to see.
It was a pillar in the community, where families met and children gathered to learn their ABCs.

I remember, with strong memories, that country school where I spent most of my elementary years.
They were days of learning, socializing and fun; heck, we even shed a few tears.

Well, it was a mile to school; many times I walked, then later rode a bike of faded red,
Or hitched a ride with Kenny on his little paint pony; and in the winter, Don picked us up in a horse-drawn sled.

We learned reading, writing, and arithmetic from one teacher for Grades One through to Eight.
She rang the bell at nine o'clock each morning and worked on her lessons into the evening late.

Yes, that one-room schoolhouse on the prairie sported chalk-boards from wall to wall.
And the learning continued into noon hours and recesses as even the teacher came out to play ball.

Auntie I over, pom-pom-pullaway, or fox and goose on a fresh snowy day;
Hopscotch, and marbles; you're it for tag, or the swings where the young ones would play.

The flag was raised every morning on that steel pole where Randy froze the tip of his tongue.
I remember Dad stopping class to show us the deer he'd just shot; over the blue Ford, the antlers they hung.

In that one-room schoolhouse on the prairie, education came in many different ways.
It didn't stop with classes; there were Halloween parties, 4-H meetings and even sports days.

And those Christmas concerts – every school district had one; neighbours from all around filled the hall.
Where everyone's son and daughter became a movie star, and Santa Claus never failed to call.

And you can't forget those country dances; the whole community came alive to the band.
With fiddle and bow, it was do si do then aleman left, hand over hand.

Then one by one, the men slipped out for a nip from Uncle's bottle; you'd tip it over to the side.
On their return, the women would scowl as they set out sandwiches, and cake they'd diligently baked with pride.

Back to the dance, the Beer Barrel Polka, the two-step with those graceful two left feet going right;
Next, the schottische and a twirl to the butterfly; then the Blue Danube waltz, a chance to snuggle up tight.

Yes, the one-room schoolhouse on the prairie became a church on Sunday morning.
Mom dressed us up in our best, we listened to Dolly do clergy, emphasizing God's revitalized warning.

During the summer, the school was scheduled for Sunday School classes for the community's young.
It was the centre for the community club, picnics, reunions; a place where many a song was sung.

Yes, those days are done; the schoolhouse is gone; education has stepped up to a faster time.
Taxes have increased; they offer classes that are spares, and the poems they teach the kids don't even rhyme.

As I seed wheat into the soil where that schoolhouse once stood, my mind often goes back in a daze,
To that one-room schoolhouse on the prairie; yes, those were the good old days.

The Swinton School enrolled children of the community from 1924 to 1962. My mother, Dorothy Burnett (Pendleton), taught there from August 1943 to June 1945.

Puppies

When God made puppies, He created fun,
A bundle of fluff and joy.
They're great for all ages, full of life,
More than just a toy.

Puppies are full of pep and ginger,
They're always on the run.
They'll lift your spirits and make you laugh,
Yes, puppies were made for fun.

Puppies bring with them a little grief
Not uncommon to the young.
Not to worry, it's overlooked
With one little slurp of the tongue.

When God made puppies, He created fun,
Cause that's just what puppies do.
It's hard enough trying to train one,
Consider managing two.

Rubber Boots

The teacher at the one-room schoolhouse had many jobs to do,
And her duties were abundant, even after the day's lessons were through.

Now when anything went astray, it always seemed that Eddy was right there.
And today his boots just didn't seem to fit – the little tyke was in despair.

So the teacher gave him a hand, she pulled and he pushed; the boots sure were tight.
By the time they got the second rubber boot on, she'd worked up a sweat alright.

When he stood up, she sighed as he exclaimed, "Teacher, they're on the wrong feet!"
Sure enough; and it wasn't any easier getting them off as he sat there on his seat.

She managed to keep her emotions under control as they pushed and pulled once more,
And together they got the boots on the right feet; Eddy grinned as his feet hit the floor.

"Ya know what, teacher?" he announced. "These really aren't my boots."
So she sat him down and started pulling the rubbers off, instead of her hair out by its roots.

The teacher struggled to yank the last boot off; her temper was about at the brim.
Then Eddy exclaimed, "They're my brother's boots, but my mother said I had to wear 'em."

Now emotions were soaring to the top; the teacher was thinking, "Do I laugh or cry?"
With what strength she had left, she pushed and pulled; the boots squeezed on with one last pry.

It was done. The rubber boots were on. She sighed, "Now, Eddy, where's your coat?"
He pointed, "It's the red one, but it's my sister's. My blue one got ate by our goat."

Finally, Eddy was at the door and the teacher was thinking, "Good riddance."
But with one last inquiry, she asked, "Eddy, now where have you put your mittens?"

Then Eddy smiled, with a twinkle in his eye, as if a switch had just turned on the light.
He said, "Oh, I forgot. I stuffed them in the toes of my boots. No wonder they fit so tight."

Young Wyatt is ready to head off for school in his rubber boots.

Saturday In Town

When I was a lad, I looked forward to Saturdays, cause that's the day the whole family went to town.
That's when Dad got repairs, Mom purchased groceries, and a boy could explore Main Street up and down.

My favourite store was Bill Chew's – The Modern News – filled with tobacco, magazines, and candy galore.
You could find most anything a boy of nine needed, with a pet shop in the back of the store.

Then around the corner was the Healy Hotel, housing a restaurant, barber shop and the biggest bar in town.
As young lads, my brother and I snuck into the hotel's elevator to catch a ride going up, then coming down.

Across the street was Ham Motors; my cousins and I looked at flat-eight motors under the hood.
Then next to it was the dentist's and doctor's clinic; going there never made me feel good.

The Paris Cafe on the corner made the best root beer floats in town.
You could twirl on a stool at the counter, or in those big red seats sink down.

There were three theatres – the Lyric, Eagles and Cinema – all with 2 o'clock matinees, popcorn, candy and fun.
By the Eagles was a drugstore; its big picture window housed a twirly thing that spun with the heat of the sun.

Quite often, Dad would visit Klings Clothing Store; the big aisles we'd follow him down.
He enjoyed visiting with Chick and Fat, who knew all the gossip going on around town.

Walkingshaw Pharmacy was Mom's preference for medicine and Buckleys mixture, which always tasted vile.
Next to it was Hall Sporting Goods and Wiskar Jewellers, where Ray met everyone with a smile.

The banks were all spread out on Main Street to facilitate merchants at little cost.
Now they're all congregated around the post office so government cheques have less time to get lost.

The final stop was Cooper Co-op where everyone met for stories to tell.
The men talked over farming and the weather, and how the world was going to hell.

Mom pushed that grocery cart up and down the aisles to get the week's food supply.
Sometimes we helped her with that hand she didn't need, making sure she got the right buy.

Then off to Grandma's; she lived above the locker plant, where we got herring that was smoked.
Then we climbed that long flight of stairs and peeked into those milk chute doors; and with Grandma's neighbours we joked.

Yes, it used to be we worked on the land all week so we could spend Saturday in town – one day filled with fun and charm.
Now we hold down a job 8-to-5 each day so we can spend Saturday home on the farm.

Our daughter Dena showing one of her heifers at a 4-H livestock event. The 4-H program enhanced Dena's ability to build a strong foundation for her future endeavours. Dena acquired degrees in both Agriculture and Engineering as well as a Masters degree in Biomedical Engineering. She is now working on her PhD. Dena helps with our annual livestock production sale every year and is proud to have ties with the ranch.

Livestock Buyers

In the profile of livestock buyers, all weren't created equal – but
you've got to give them some slack.
Good ones are few and far between, like a cow's upper teeth –
not up front but grinding you hard in the back.

Now livestock buyers don't like many calves; they sort them and
say things that are mean.
"When the calf was born, the cow should have eaten it instead of
licking it clean."

What they want you don't have, you're always two years behind,
your cows sure ain't bred the right way.
They're always the wrong colour, too heavy or too light, and the
price just fell yesterday.

Livestock buyers don't know what a good cow looks like, and no
cow makes the right kind of steer.
They try to buy them for less and sell them for more, and the
margins change with each bottle of beer.

If you have white calves, they want tans; and if you've got tans,
they're probably looking for black.
When they've got a white face, a bronco or blaze would be
better; and they don't like a stripe down their back.

It depends whether they're buying or selling, what packages fit,
and if they had to sort in the mud.
When they're buying calves, your cows should be coyote bait or
the bull you used was a dud.

But when they're selling your calves, it's another story; to their
buyers, they're portrayed like peas in a pod.
They've sorted and mixed them, put in some good ones and
taken out the ones that were odd.

It makes one wonder when cattle buyers were born if their mothers
kept them clean, just like a momma cow licks off her calf,
Or if their diapers got shortchanged and now they're shortchanging
us, and are finally getting the last laugh.

Parts

A lady on the farm can be invaluable, especially at the busiest time of the season.
She's often willing to do her part, running here and there for almost any reason.

But things changed one day when one lady was summoned to do a particular chore.
A breakdown had occurred; would she make a trip to town to go to the machinery parts store?

So she walked into the store and waited in line; it would soon be her turn, then she'd be on her way.
The parts man greeted her, "Well, howdy, madam; and how can I help you today?"

She said, "I need a thingamajig for that whatchamacallit that runs on that old hunk of tin.
I hope you got it; my husband needs it so he can get the crop in the bin."

Well, the parts man slapped his hand to his head, smiled once and gave a blank look.
"What machine's it on, what's the make and the model so we can look it up in the book?"

She said, "It's on a combine that's red and it's got a number nine; oh, and it's got a white top."
"Well, now we're cooking, madam. Is it on the drive shaft – maybe a bearing with a collar that makes it stop?"

It took them a while but they narrowed it down to something that runs on a little round pipe.
They were still not sure if it was from the front or the back, but were darn sure it was the turning type.

"So, madam, how's it held on – with an Allen screw or maybe a Woodruff key?"
"No, my husband's name's not Allen or Woodrow, but some baling wire I did see."

"So, madam, what size does it fit – the dimension, the diameter of that shaft?"
She held up her hand, "It's about this big around." But it didn't help when he turned his back and laughed.

"Well, I'm sorry, madam, but we're going to have to order it in, cause there's nothing here with that dimension."
That's when the bubble burst – she couldn't take it in anymore; she'd been holding in the tension.

She said, "Mister, you can take that thingamajig along with that combine and shove it up your butt."
"Well, I'm sorry, madam, but there ain't no room – I got a rake and a baler shoved up there this morning and now it just won't shut."

So all you ladies, when you go to town for parts, just be sure to take along the broken bit.
When they say they have to order it in, then they laugh and turn their backs, you can make sure it's a custom fit.

Gone Fishing

When the westerly winds sift soft white snow through slopes dividing Duncairn Dam,
The fishermen frolic, forming holes in the ice through which hooks they hopefully cram.

Dave and Campbell were fishing buddies who often frequented there, giving those fish a try.
The only day that they couldn't be found fishing was on days that didn't end in a 'Y'.

Now Dave had an ice auger propelled by a motor that was darn near plum worn out.
He bustled around drilling holes all over the dam; yes, he was a fishing scout.

Campbell, he just sat at the first hole dug, dropped his line and waited for fish to bite.
He'd drag them in and fill a pail; he'd sit there morning 'til night.

But Dave, he liked to see how the neighbours were doing; and he sold wildlife memberships.
He knew who was catching all the fish and he was always willing to relay his fishing tips.

And when he hooked a fish, he let everyone know how big it was as out the line ran.
He enjoyed a good fight and would exclaim, "Keep 'em as big as you dare as long as you can!"

But Campbell on the other hand brought them in quick without much fuss and holler,
Explaining, "You can't let them fight cause they lose weight, and then it seems they get smaller."

When the day was done they always talked over their trip, with a draft of Hudson's Bay Rum.
Then they'd retire to bed, dreaming of that big perch they'd eventually catch in days to come.

As winter winds whistle snow over Duncairn Dam, it seems to softly whisper the names
Of the two old boys who frequented its ice-covered waters, immersed in those frivolous fishing games.

My father, David Burnett, was an avid fisherman and outdoorsman. He enjoyed it when fish put up a good fight.
A favourite expression of his was: "Keep them as big as you dare as long as you can."

More Memories Than Dreams

A young lad fitted on his boots and cowboy hat, positioned his badge as he opened the door.
He grasped the reins of his broomstick horse as he galloped across the deck floor.

He nudged the old man being hugged by a chair, his chin tucked tight to his chest.
"Wake up, Grandpa! Are you dreaming dreams or are your eyes just having a rest?"

A raspy voice retorted, "Dreams … I can tell you dreams. See, I once had a horse like that.
It was a wooden rocking horse that your great grandpa made; proudly on it I sat.

That horse and I, we once rode together, pounded dirt and rocked through many a year.
On top of that steed I roped rank renegades, and in a rodeo he'd buck and rear.

We chased those outlaws, moving hard and fast; we set a frisky pace.
That horse was a champion, that's for sure; he always won the race.

We scouted out Jesse James and Geronimo – made 'em run with a yip and a whoop.
Then we team-roped in that arena, headed and healed all with only one loop.

On that wood floor, we dragged calves for banding; even challenged a charging bull.
We corralled white-faced heifers in record time, and even competed in a heavy horse pull."

Now toy ponies, they gallop on forever – but young cowboys not so much.
Wooden horses and championship ribbons are set aside for grown-up things and such.

No one really knows how it happens – growing cowboys gradually spread their wings.
Sheriff badges, outlaws, and six shooters are abandoned to corral other things.

So ride that horse hard – let her buck – over rolling hills that are forever wild.
Shake out a loop and lasso the stars before you're no longer a child.

Gather in your dreams and cinch 'em up tight, then ride 'em for all they are worth,
Cut them out fast from the billowing clouds and to a memory you'll give birth.

So as I sit here, am I dreaming dreams? Nah. You see, that's what grandsons are for.
They're no longer dreams, merely memories … more memories than dreams anymore.

This young cowboy is a typical sight at local rodeo events.

Life, Love and Laughter

As we journey through our daily rituals and flirt with life's many obstacles, it is important to take some comfort in the lighter side of living. Life is what happens as we make our way through this world trying to accomplish our goals, fulfill our dreams and keep the coyotes at bay.

In him was life, and life was the light of men. And the light shineth in darkness, and the darkness comprehended it not. (John 1)

Oh, but to take life's light and fill the darkness with love and laughter. We could be so blessed to rejoice and enjoy those happy, fruitful moments which enrich our lives.

Now, on another aspect to life's moments ... I remember being told that many a great cowboy poem has two basic ingredients – disaster and time. What once happened as an unfortunate incident can over a period of time render a story, flirting with humour and humility – sometimes based on fact, sometimes an exaggeration, and sometimes it's just appropriate not to let the truth get in the way of a good story.

You may surrender to the conclusion, as I have on various occasions, that laughter could be the cure for what ails ya.

Three Good Things

They say a cowboy should be fulfilled if he's had but three things in his life;
One a good horse, another a good dog, and the last – a great loving wife.

A good horse – guess I've had one, cause she knew more about cows than I;
She could bring in the whole herd all by herself, and loved it if a critter tried to sneak by.

But the best horse we had was a little grey pony that I never really rode at all,
Her hooves grew too long and she travelled real slow, accompanying our kids at their every call.

And I've had many a dog – enjoyed them all, as abundant memories they made.
A golden lab shared my boyhood adventures; in companionship, we hunted and played.

A Blue Heeler, Australian Shepherd and a Cocker Spaniel all were special to me,
But a little Pomeranian stole my heart, as her tricks she performed with glee.

And a good wife – well, how can I compare; I've only had but one.
I can't imagine having any more than that; gosh, a man ain't supposed to have that much fun.

Well, I know she's not perfect; she's got her faults – after all, she married me,
But I can't hold that against her cause I ain't perfect either, and that's easy for her to see.

She's been with me all these years and put up with my shenanigans, even when I embarrass her with a poem like this.
So I guess you could say I've had one good wife; least ways she sure reminds me of that whenever her dinners I miss.

So I guess you could say my life has been fulfilled, but it is all because of my wife, don't you see;
Cause she's the one who brought home that little grey pony and the Pomeranian, and if I remember right – heck, she's the one who proposed to me.

Our son Wyatt spending time with the grey pony Mitsy.

My niece Shara and Brent Lunn were married in the Peace River country of Alberta. The poem Matrimonial Bliss was presented to them at the ceremony. Although it stormed and rained all day, they got the job done.

Matrimonial Bliss

The cowboy and the lady returning from their honeymoon, settled down to make his house their home.
She would share his life, domestication on track; no more would he have to roam.

Many months of matrimonial bliss rolled by, then they realized finances were tougher than during their single days.
So she studied the cheque ledger, trying to decide how they could mend their ways.

To her husband she said, "Last week, you spent twenty dollars on beer. We can do without that, you know."
Then he noticed the eighty-five dollars spent on makeup and replied, "Well, what the heck, that can go."

She flashed a sexy smile and a twinkle suddenly sparkled from her eyes of blue,
"I put on makeup for your benefit, darling, so I look prettier for you."

He replied, "Honey, we don't need to spend money on makeup so you look better for me to adore.
You see, dear, we can save that money, cause that's what the beer is for."

Now he's thinking he should have been a bit easier on her and where her thoughts were coming from,
Cause she took her makeup, their cheque book and his beer to spend some quality time with her mom.

You Could Be A Cowboy If

You could be a cowboy if your dog gets to ride in the pickup truck more than your wife,
Or if you've cleaned your horse's hoof, then sliced up an apple – all with your castrating knife.

You could be a cowboy if you've driven like hell for eight hours, then prayed you could make an eight-second ride, escaping death,
Or whispered to your horse, praised your dog, and scowled at your woman all in the very same breath.

As an old cowboy, you may recall when 'topless' meant going around without your hat on for a while,
Or when your teeth and the truck door both displayed that same Copenhagen smile.

You may qualify if there's more money on the console of your pickup truck than in your bank account,
But when it's your turn to a buy a round for the rodeo gals, seems you've got any amount.

You could be a cowboy if you've been known to cut barbed wire with your teeth, or pull down a bull with a nose hold,
You've been vaccinated against blackleg and anthrax, you've been deloused and dewormed, but can't seem to shake the common cold.

As a cowboy you'll never admit that you're lost – you've just misplaced yourself wherever,
And when asked to produce I.D., you show your name on the back of your belt engraved in cowhide leather.

You could be a cowboy if you've listened to coyotes yip in the dead of night, then joined and howled at the moon,
Or poured one last cup of coffee as the campfire flickers, and strummed your guitar as you sang out of tune.

You could be a cowboy if you stand big and tall, and at tough guys try not to appear weak,
But you sure qualify if you've buried your favourite old dog and tears rolled down your cheek.

You could be a cowboy if no matter where or how far you wander or roam,
You can humbly kneel and praise God up above, knowing this is only your temporary home.

Life's Role

The cowboy and his newlywed bride rolled up in a red river cart.
Their homestead in sight; fresh air, fresh water and a fresh start.

Their ranch grew fast, with cattle, horses and forage crops to seed.
Three years rolled by and they were blessed with three little mouths to feed.

That wasn't enough, so they settled right in and soon gave birth to three more.
The first three were boys, then came three girls to even out the score.

They had produced an even half dozen, and were challenged to feed the crew.
Mom just got a dozen of everything, then every child could have two.

Soon these six were grown up and having young ones of their own.
And so it is that generations roll on; that's how family trees are grown.

It seems life resembles a roll of toilet paper, as the years swiftly flow,
Cause the closer we get to the end of our role, the faster it seems to go.

Steak House

"The grub looks great," the cowboy thought as he was escorted to a table.
The waiter poured some water, then proudly pointed to the menu label.

"Welcome to our establishment," he said. "It's a pleasure to serve you, Monsieur.
By the cut of your clothes and that cowboy hat, I take it you're a steak connoisseur.

We offer a porterhouse steak, eight-ounce prime rib, or a twelve if you so wish,
Two sizes of sirloin, New York cut, or filet mignon with baked potato side dish.

We can cook them well done, medium rare or even easy over,
Smothered with mushrooms, salsa sauce or bacon bits with a sprig of parsley clover."

The cowboy ordered his favourite steak and anticipated his meal,
When a tall gentleman sat down at the next table, looking lost and somewhat surreal.

The waiter approached and said, "Welcome, sir. Can we order you a steak today?"
His complexion was pale as the man replied, "Just a tossed salad will be okay."

The waiter whispered to the cowboy, as he gave his own shoulders a shrug,
"Ordering a salad in a steak house is kind of like asking a hooker for a hug."

Silent Is Golden

The cowboy and a lady strutted into the lounge, and at an elaborately set table they sat.
The setting was perfect, fit for a queen; heck, he even took off his hat.

They ordered a drink and settled right in; yes, this could be the start of a new romance,
She laughed at his stories – he had style – as she gave him that little-girl glance.

Things seemed perfect, then a pungent odour cut the air, like a knife shearing your very soul.
"Excuse me," she gasped, "I'm passing gas, and can't seem to keep it under control."

The waiter appeared and waved his hand through the smog, giving the cowboy a defiant look.
He smiled at the lady, saying, "Can I take your order?" – then wrote it down in his book.

When the waiter left, the lady uttered, "Oh, I just let a couple silent ones go, and I really don't know what to do."
The cowboy smiled. "Well, for a start," he said, "I'd get my hearing checked if I was you."

Aging

As years roll by, they surely increase one's apprehension of being inspired.
But the older we get, we realize it takes longer to rest up than it did to get tired.

In our later life, it seems that we fill precious time we longingly did crave.
Wanting to find something to do with the time, we've rushed through life trying to save.

As we go through life, age makes us feel somewhat bolder,
Cause no matter how old we get, there's always someone who looks older.

We must be careful what we say; we ain't as strong as when we were young.
Remember we're for sure older than our teeth, but not any older than our tongue.

Now the older we get, the more knowledge we're able to embrace,
Which is eagerly enhanced if wisdom can just put it properly in its place.

And most important is something that we surely don't want to forget;
Age is a fascinating thing, as the older we are, it seems the older we want to get.

Later Life

In later life, when the lust for love lingers at a long-lasting low,
A lady looks in the mirror, which reflects a loss of her youthful glow.

Her fingers press against the glass, sketching facial features weathered by life's storms.
Grey and silver tint her once golden brown hair, as she studies a faded form.

She looks at the cowboy as he lies on the bed and a tear comes to her eye.
She says, "I don't like the reflections I see in the mirror; they're different than days gone by.

My eyes have bags, my cheeks have sags, and my chin is folded in double time.
Some parts droop and others bulge; all were once firm in my prime.

It reflects a body that's been aged with time; things were different in my younger days.
Console me, dear; please tell me something is right, please offer me some praise."

Now the cowboy looked at his aged mate who was once his beautiful bride.
She struggles now, but his love is still strong; he'll remain faithful by her side.

He longingly looked at his lifelong love; how could he lessen her lamented call?
Finally he smiled as he replied, "Well, one thing's for certain, dear. Your eyesight ain't failed you at all."

Twins

The old cowboy decided to do his civic duty and take tickets for the rodeo.
He greeted the oncoming crowd: "Howdy, folks. Welcome and enjoy the show."

All went well, then he saw her coming – mean and ugly, cussing her children up and down.
Why, if a Brahma bull could see her, he'd sure enough paw the ground.

The closer she got, the meaner she looked, and hollering at those kids every which way.
The cowboy greeted her, "Hello, madam. Can I get tickets for you and your twins today?"

She scowled. "What the heck do you think? 'Course I want tickets, you moron.
And what makes you think these are twins? One's eight, the other's ten. Is your brain completely gone?"

The cowboy smiled, handed over the tickets and said, "My mistake. Sorry if I appear a bit naive.
But for you to trick a man into bed more than once – that's pretty hard to believe."

Don Johnson (left), longtime friend of my father-in-law Woodrow Newton, enjoying talking over old times with my brother-in-law Wade Newton.

Wyatt tries his hand at fishing on the big rocks at
Reindeer Lake, Saskatchewan.

Fishing

As the sun does glisten on the water, if you listen,
you can hear two old boys start to talk.
From home they were missing, cause they were out a fishing,
stretched out on that big black rock.

Mac said, “Boy, this is fun, lying out in the sun,
just waiting for the big one to bite.
The only thing I never done was let my wife know where I’ve gone;
she’ll be nattering at me all the night.”

Judd replied, “Mine said fishing is a waste, as I left the house in haste;
funny how women have their ways.
I might just leave the place, and by herself her life she’ll face,
cause she ain’t going to talk to me for days.”

Mac took a sip of his brew, then he repositioned his chew,
and gave his reel a short wind.
He said, “If I was only you, I’d reconsider my view,
cause a woman like that is mighty hard to find.”

Cowboys And Grease Guns

The government said, "Boys, it's time to register your guns, whether you want to or not."
So I grabbed the old grease gun and thought, "Register this – it's the most dangerous gun we've got."

See, cowboys and grease zerks aren't overly compatible, and that's when one must refrain,
Cause trying to shoot a grease zerk with that old grease gun can drive a cowboy insane.

I unholster that gun and it works just fine until there's about three zerks left to go.
That's when the gun runs out of grease; she's empty, wouldn't you know.

When a cartridge is changed in a grease gun, one must sit back and regress,
Cause when a cowboy dismantles a grease gun, one of them's going to end up a mess.

Pants and shirt become a grease rag by the time the gun's back together.
With a couple of pumps, a gob of grease lands on my new boot leather.

Then back under the machine to find the grease zerks; only two left, then we're done.
With two pumps it develops an air lock, so it's back up to bleed the darn gun.

Loosen her off and out comes the air, squirting grease onto my nose.
Shirt sleeves become a rag then; wouldn't you know – there's a kink in the rubber hose.

That last zerk is always the hardest to get at, and why it doesn't take grease finally appears.
Now it seems I've been trying to grease a quarter-inch bolt for at least the last couple of years.

So there's one thing for certain; cowboys and grease guns sure are accustomed to battle,
And I know I'll be leaving this outfit if they ever fit a grease zerk onto my saddle.

A cowboy's dream – no grease zerks!

The Tale Of The Bull Ride

As the night does decay into the edge of the next day,
and the whiskey wisdom starts to prevail,
A cowboy's belly caresses the bar, his buddies listen from afar;
he says, "Tis time to tell you a tale.

Reckon I'll relate to you a phrase about my rodeo days,
when I drew the bull they call The Brute.
He could turn left or right, then blow up like dynamite
as he kicked out with a blast and a toot.

I straddled his back and pulled up the slack
from the rope wrapped around his chest.
He lunged at the chute, that bull called The Brute,
just a hankering to show me his best.

The gate swung open wide and he stood there with pride,
then promptly all four feet left the ground.
He crashed down with a thud, through the muck and the mud,
then suddenly started spinning around.

I gritted my teeth and held on, for beneath
was a ton of raging fury on the fight.
He slipped to the side and never broke stride
when my head struck his hip in full flight.

Well, his tail swiped my face and his switch it was placed
directly between my front teeth.
I chomped down with a grip when he came up with his hip,
and the rope came loose from beneath.

My feet hit the ground, as my teeth clenched down
on the tail of the one called The Brute.
With his horns drawing near and my face stuck at his rear,
we made circles in front of the chute.

On about the fifth pass, he started passing out gas;
my teeth they bit down in despair,
My eyes started to blink; recycled grasses sure stink
and the aroma, it hung in the air.

Oh, he snorted and twirled as around him he hurled
this cowboy and his teeth filled with plaque.
Then from under his tail hair came one final blast of foul air,
and he stopped right there in his track.

Well, he collapsed to the ground, as the clowns gathered 'round,
and from my teeth I set that bull loose.
Now the crowd, they did cheer for the cowboy who did appear
to have tamed that wild cayuse."

The cowboy poured a beer, celebrating the tale his buddies did hear,
as he raised to them his glass.
But if the truth be complete, that bull wasn't beat;
The Brute merely just ran out of gas.

This photo was taken at the Swift Current Frontier Days Rodeo.
The 75th Frontier Days was held in 2013. (Used with permission.)

Summoning Spirit And Soul

In the beginning, God created the heaven and the earth. (Genesis 1)

Now there are those who subscribe to a different version – the big bang theory – that all was created with a huge big bang and the miracles of life burst forth. Well, I have come to the conclusion in my warped sort of analysis that maybe both occurred and it could be written as such – *in the beginning, there was a big bang as God created the heaven and the earth.*

I have been fortunate to live a life on the land, at Mother Nature's very doorstep. Every day, I witness God's many creations and their effects on my livelihood, being and spirit; the consequence being a rewarding stewardship between the land, its creatures and caretakers. Every year for the last forty years, we have had fifty to one hundred first-calf heifers calve in February. There have been many nights on the 3:00 a.m. trek back to the house that I looked up at the dimly lit moon and the infinite stars and said, "Thank you, God, for allowing me to do what I do." There is great satisfaction observing the miracle of birth; a being from within, the first breath, the realization of life and a caring mother. A big bang? I don't think so.

I hope you will enjoy and be touched by these poems which explore the meaning, comprehend the existence, and offer praise for the fortunes of a life lived close to the land and summoned by Mother Nature's call.

Last Ride

I hold my head straight and proud,
my life has been well blessed.
For soon my spirit will be set free
and my body laid to rest.

I've fulfilled a cowboy's dream;
galloped over open spaces.
Gazed in wonder at the sun's rise and set,
chased the day through its paces.

I've trailed in many a bred heifer
down the wandering fence line.
And claimed the odd fancy filly
from the Master's herd as mine.

As I depart, I beg to ask,
kindly overlook my pride.
A last request, Lord – if you could see fit,
please grant me one last ride.

Angel

They say a baby is a bundle of joy sent down from up above.
A miracle in its mother's arms, a testament of love.

Before embarking on its earthly journey, a question is asked by the newborn,
Saying, "God, how will I know what to do when I arrive, lost and somewhat forlorn?

Who will be there to comfort me, guide me and help me along?"
God replied, "I'll send you an angel to whisper your name and sing to you a song."

The newborn said, "But I will be so small and fragile; are you sure I'll be okay?"
God replied, "Yes, my child. My angel will watch over you at night and every day."

"But God, I don't understand the earthly language and how to communicate."
God replied, "Be still, my child. The angel I send will teach you to relate."

"And when I need you, God, how will I know where you are and what to say?"
God replied, "Oh, child, my angel will appear and show you how to pray."

"But God, how will I recognize this angel and where it does come from?"
"Fear not, my child, the angel will appear upon your birth. Look up and call her 'Mom'."

The Meaning

I met a cowboy outside a store one day,
whittling on a hunk of wood.
I asked him of philosophy, life's events
and what made great times really good.

He said, "Son, life is like shaping this old chunk of wood
from one end to the other.
It's got to be sculpted with the proper tools,
starting with a father and a mother.

People spend money they don't have on things they don't need
to impress folks they don't even know.
They forget life's meaning – family, God, a dog for a friend,
and taking time to watch kids grow.

God made man and woman to join together, create a family,
carrying one generation into another.
It's important when raising kids to give them someone to look up to
and be proud of – a dad and a mother.

Children need time to play, dream and fantasize,
to walk with Mother Nature while they can.
Don't rush them to get old and be tempted with worldly ways;
you'll blink and a boy has changed into a man.

You have to enjoy life, shape it the proper way,
make sure all the pieces tightly fit.
You can't buy your way through; money won't buy happiness,
it just lets you explore more for it.

Most important is integrity and truth, don't shortchange yourself;
above all, be faithful to the core.
There are no sure shortcuts; stand proud and strong,
and leave the devil knocking at the door.

When you shape your life, whittle it true and straight;
don't give in to the jeering of the crowd.
Remember your parents and the love of God above;
be sure that in you they would be proud."

Have You Bin There

Have you bin there at the break of dawn when the sun was peeking through the sky,
And pondered its golden brilliance, then stopped to wonder why?

Why is it that all this wondrous creation is here for us to see,
And why is it that most don't appreciate it near as much as me?

Have you bin there in spring when the prairie soil warmed, letting purple crocuses grow,
And you fixed the wire fence that was pulled down from ice and melting snow?

Have you bin there as a momma cow nuzzled her calf, her tongue caressing it into life,
Then watched another push her lifeless calf in despair, bellowing in tormented strife?

Have you bin there checking cows, on a mare you've been breaking, figuring her confidence you finally did win,
Then she spooked, threw you off; a leg was broken and darkness settled in?

Have you bin there when crops were three feet tall and one more rain would yield a bumper crop to flail,
Then the clouds burst forth, and your heart jumped with joy – but with the rain also came hail?

Have you bin there as your son and his pup played fetch, and ran and jumped with glee,
Then with tears in your eyes, cradled your favourite old dog as he laid lifeless over your knee?

Have you bin there as autumn regressed, left behind by the beauty and smell of fresh falling snow,
Then your fingers turned numb and your cheeks and nose froze when it hit 30 below?

Have you bin there and watched your parents gracefully age and share their love with you,
Then endured the hardships and felt the pain when there were no longer two?

Have you bin there and watched a loved one suffer, lying in that hospital bed,
And prayed, "Oh God, how can this be, if only it were me instead?"

Have you bin there and attended the miracle of birth, a life squeezed into this world,
The feeling of wonder, astonishment and awe, as a new beginning unfurled?

Why is it man takes life for granted, mutilates and kills with greed?
Why can't we realize that harmony and love, and peace is what we need?

Well, if you've bin there through life's joys and struggles, and find it hard to understand,
Then compassion and peace are truly yours when you put your trust in God's loving hand.

My Religious Cow

Calving season's near done; all the cows that are left are only a few.
The Almighty must've been watching over 'em; think we've only lost but two.

One day, checking cows, Number 10 ran towards me – bellering and carrying on.
She gave a long bellow then turned around, headed out, and she was gone.

Her udder was tight – she hadn't been sucked – and I decided to follow along.
She stopped between two hills, stood there a calling; I knew that something was wrong.

Right by the fence, she stood and mooed while a coyote viewed the scene.
Now I figured either he got her calf or it was in the neighbour's pasture in a ravine.

I scouted the pasture, looking for that calf, but my search was all in vain.
I returned to the cow, still calling for her baby – it seemed she was in such pain.

I said, "Sorry, girl, I can't find your calf," then I glanced down at her feet.
The calf's hind leg stuck out of a badger hole; it was wedged in that retreat.

I tugged on the leg, then started to dig, trying to get it free.
I yanked the calf out – its neck was bent, but it was alive as could be.

It struggled to its feet, as the cow mothered it up, ceasing her anguished beller.
I said, "You're welcome, girl; you'll be fine, so take care of that little feller."

On the evening check, they looked okay; then I noticed a halo beamed around cow Number 10.
See, she bore a calf, then I pulled it from a badger hole – you could say it was born again.

A Black Angus cow-calf pair just prior to weaning in the fall.

Succession

Some refer to it as the changing of the guard; the old model exchanged for the new.
And it will eventually transpire, even though I'm not anxious for it to.
So why does it have to be so complicated to move along with my life?
Seems that I'm just like old Mother Earth, moulded with toil and strife.
This rich soil will soon consume me, covered up in gravel and grit.
But just settle back – let's reminisce – cause I just ain't ready yet.

These years creep up on a guy; one wonders where they all went.
But this old ranch has been good to me; I've been grateful for the years I've spent.
In these last few years, I've been slowing down; it's been tough on this old pup.
My mind's still thinking that I'm young, but this old body just can't keep up.
So they're telling me it's time to step aside, retire and never fret,
But I don't know, it just don't seem right – cause I just ain't ready yet.

This land has been real fruitful to me; it'll grow grass with a bit of rain.
Our cows are fat and the crop's in the bin; we're good for the year again.
As I survey this ranch – all I've accomplished – years garnished with toil and sweat,
My body is broken and my mind meanders, but I just ain't ready yet.

My wife figures we should move to town, settle in an old folks' home.
Where I'd be content in a four-walled suite with only the front lawn to roam.
She says it would be nice and relaxing; I could sleep and coffee all day.

She wouldn't have to make any meals and her video games she could play.
It could be a gated community; she's thinking the bars would retain me, I'll bet.
Well, that might be pleasing to her, but I just ain't ready yet.

So I take a drive in my old pickup truck; all this thinking requires fresh air.
It's out to the pasture to check the herd, let the wind caress my sparse hair.
There he is, the bull – our herd sire going on for the sixth season.
His calves always push the scale to the top; he's survived for the right reason.
He's left his mark on our herd; his daughters are the best we could ever get.
Just like him, I don't want to retire, cause I just ain't ready yet.

We've been trying to do some future planning; they refer to it as succession.
I got a lawyer hired to figure it out; costs a lot for the legal profession.
They say we got to get it down right and proper, so there's nothing we'll later regret.
But I'm not really sure of this procedure, cause I just ain't ready yet.

That darn succession – I detest that word, cause I know it refers to the end.
Or maybe in a way it's a new beginning, with the next generation around the bend.
But, either way, it refers to planning, and a cowboy prefers to procrastinate.
Though I probably should sit down and get it on paper before it is too late.
So here I am with pen in hand; my mind's racing lest I forget.
But how can I get it all wrote down – I just ain't ready yet.

I enjoy working alongside my son and pushing this ranch along.
He's got a good handle on what this ranch can do – separate the right from the wrong.
My son, he's chomping at the bit; he's ready to run the race.
It seems sometimes I'm holding him back, trying to keep a steady pace.

I've been thinking I should cut him loose, let him carry the bulk of the debt.
But that's a big weight to bear and besides, I ain't sure if he's ready yet.

They say all good things eventually come to an end, or do we just start over again?
When it's passed on to the next generation, is a new chapter at the end of the lane?
So is there a plan in this old world, how things get moved along,
A divine intervention to an ultimate goal, keeping generations strong?
God has a plan for our succession, our Saviour is the one we must not forget.
For when he reappears, we best not say, "I just ain't ready yet."

We were proud to be presented with the Century Family Farm Award for both the Burnett and Pendleton sides of the family. The award is for families that have continuously farmed the land for 100 years. The Burnett and Pendleton farms are now moving on to the fourth generation.

Destiny

Does a man carve out his own destiny
from that of life's path he does take?
And is it from the many good deeds he's done
or from one bad mistake?

Is man's destiny like a feather floating in the breeze,
challenged for somewhere to land?
Or is it shaped by that of a Superior Being,
ever there with a guiding hand?

Maybe it's a little of both, a mixture,
like a roll of the dice,
Then the guidance of a shepherd's cane pulling us in
instead of rolling twice.

And how are we to know what's in store for us;
what's waiting around the bend?
How we behold our body may reveal a longer life,
or a quicker rush to the end.

Now maybe man's destiny was made for him
by another's hands of fate,
All man's destiny was sealed by a woman
when the apple Eve regretfully ate.

Wanda and the Blue Heeler pup Rosie at Narrarrwhurrut Station, Australia. In the early 1980s, we ventured into a partnership in a cattle property in Australia. It was truly a lifetime adventure full of challenges, commitment and success. Many great memories remain.

Producer's Prayer

God, I offer you this simple, humble prayer,
as the faith of those around us is growing dim.
Please open your arms and forgive me, Lord,
for I do believe in Him.

Oh, I know church ain't been the first on my list,
but I've had Your whole world in which to pray.
Often times I've stopped and given thanks for Your creations,
cause they're right in front of me every day.

I've wondered in awe as I planted seeds in the soil,
how with the rain You make them grow.
And when I watched a momma nuzzle her newborn calf,
Lord, it just set my heart to glow.

Lord, I've marvelled at the brilliance as Your new day dawns,
and worked well past the warmth of Your setting sun.
It's been a pleasure riding alongside old Mother Nature;
sure, we've had our toils, but mostly, Lord, it's been fun.

I've been fortunate, I guess, working close to my roots;
but maybe it's right next to our very beginning.
I've helped produce food to feed the world and though the prices
haven't been all that great, the satisfaction seems quite fitting.

Well, we're a productive bunch, Lord, producing more than we
need, and sometimes it seems like we're just giving it away.
But it never seemed to bother us none cause we just offer our
praise, and figure that next year will bring us a better day.

So I thank you, Lord; and please continue to bless my good
works, until the two of us finally meet;
Then just let me rest my bedroll not by Your side, Lord,
but merely at Your feet.

Treasure The Moment

Have you treasured the moment – knowing the world spins so fast, if it stopped you'd be thrown off?
Have you wondered in awe at God's creations while others pass by and scoff?

Have you grasped a fist full of rich Mother Earth ready to burst forth new life,
Or watched loving arms cradle your child, and you thanked God for your loving wife?

Have you taken in the aroma of freshly washed sheets billowing on a clothesline,
Or watched as a breeze floats up a feather, then whispers through the pine?

Have you held toboggan ropes in your hands as Venus twinkles through a blue frosty haze,
And treasured the moment of one last ride, then homeward bound over snow-covered ways?

Have you smelled the fragrance of a spring rain, promising a better year will come to pass;
The anticipation of an abundant hay crop with the aroma of freshly cut grass?

Have you watched a bee buzz from flower to flower and then hum its way back to its hive,
Or stood on a hill by a stone-covered grave and wondered of the view when he was alive?

Have you tiptoed over teepee rings and imagined the beating of a distant drum,
Or marvelled at a stone hammer head, contemplating its creation before white man had come?

Have you admired a new foal on wobbly legs, safe by its mother's side,
Then laughed as it raced alongside a butterfly, stronger with every stride?

Have you wondered in awe as a calf drew its first breath,
the miracle of new life;
Then cradled your lifeless old dog with trembling arms,
a true friend through joy and strife?

Have you looked up in the night at the dimly lit moon and marvelled
at the infinity of the stars?
Is your life closing in on the end or only touching the beginning;
will your soul soar past Jupiter and Mars?

My friend, if you can treasure these moments and realize that
God has a handle on it all,
Then you are fortunate to have lived a life close to the land and
summoned to Mother Nature's call.

Summoning Spirit And Soul

May I reverently reflect upon life's journey
as I turn its every page.
When the last chapter is read and the cover folded,
may I realize a graceful age.

May I be tempted with fulfillment,
but fail to outsmart my common sense.
As the force of gravity pulls me down,
may God's mercy raise me above the fence.

When my soul will pass through the Great Divide,
do not grieve for me,
For I will accompany the sun's rays that brightly shine,
and the wind you cannot see.

I will pierce the shrill of a coyote's howl
in the stillness of the night,
And slide on the sparkle of a star that ever shines so bright.

I will cling to the moist cluster of freshly fallen snow,
And frolic with a feather floating on the winds that blow.

I'll caress the first breath a calf inhales,
creating determination in its eye.
May I pollinate a butterfly's wing as it flutters through the sky.

I'll bask in the warm spring soil and push forth crocuses to grow.
Then cinch onto a warm summer breeze and flirt with wheat
heads of golden glow.

Weep not for me but for yourself,
that you could engage life such as I,
For light has shone brightly for me on earth,
as it will when I reach the sky.

When the last page is turned, the light flickers and fades
as I attain my final goal,
May my faith prevail, forgiveness granted,
and summoning of spirit and soul.

The last one through the Pearly Gates left them open for me and for you.

(Photo by Just-A-Few Fotos.)

About The Author

Bryce Burnett is a rancher, cowboy poet and entertainer from southwest of Swift Current, Saskatchewan. He and his wife Wanda, daughter Wadena, son Wyatt and daughter-in-law Chelsey operate Burnett Angus and Tarentaise, raising purebred and commercial cattle. They have had a successful cattle production sale every April for the past 30 years.

Bryce obtained his Bachelor of Science degree in Agriculture in 1972 at the University of Saskatchewan, although some say he hides it well. He is more at home working with cattle and checking crops than punching a computer keyboard.

The ranch headquarters are situated on the quarter section of land that his grandfather Walter Burnett homesteaded in 1907. The view from the kitchen window of Bryce and Wanda's semi-underground house overlooks the spot where Walter Burnett established his sod shack 100-plus years ago. The ranch and farm are now being passed to the fourth generation as Wyatt is grasping the reins and making many of the operation's decisions.

Bryce has always had a fondness for the great outdoors. As a boy, it wasn't unusual for him to have pets of rabbits, squirrels, foxes, ducks and salamanders – occasionally, many at the same time. Some of his fondest memories are chasing an old yellow dog up and down coulees of the Swift Current Creek, hunting pheasants with his father David.

Bryce has performed throughout Western Canada and in the United States at cowboy poetry gatherings and as an entertainer for livestock events, banquets and social functions. He has entertained at Canadian Western Agribition, Calgary Stampede and Rodeo, and the National Western Stock Show. His writings, stories and poetry are authentic to the life he lives on the ranch and depict so-called acquaintances who have inspired him.